Soccer Superstar
Lionel Messi

by Jon M. Fishman

LERNER PUBLICATIONS ◆ MINNEAPOLIS

Note to Educators

Throughout this book, you'll find critical-thinking questions. These can be used to engage young readers in thinking critically about the topic and in using the text and photos to do so.

Lerner Publications Company
A division of Lerner Publishing Group, Inc.
241 First Avenue North
Minneapolis, MN 55401 USA

For reading levels and more information, look up this title at www.lernerbooks.com.

Main body text set in Helvetica Textbook Com Roman 23/49.
Typeface provided by Linotype AG.

Library of Congress Cataloging-in-Publication Data

Names: Fishman, Jon M., author
Title: Soccer superstar Lionel Messi / by Jon M. Fishman.
Description: Minneapolis : Lerner Publications, [2020] | Series: Bumba books. Sports superstars | Includes
    bibliographical references and index. | Audience: Age 4–7. | Audience: K to Grade 3.
Identifiers: LCCN 2018050532 (print) | LCCN 2018055011 (ebook) | ISBN 9781541576759 (eb pdf) |
    ISBN 9781541576735 (lib) | ISBN 9781541576742 (pbk)
Subjects: LCSH: Messi, Lionel, 1987–—Juvenile literature. | Soccer players—Argentina—Biography—Juvenile
    literature.
Classification: LCC GV942.7.M398 (ebook) | LCC GV942.7.M398 F574 2020 (print) | DDC 796.334092 [B]—dc23

LC record available at https://lccn.loc.gov/2018050532

Manufactured in the United States of America
1-46631-47629-1/14/2019

Table of Contents

Soccer Hero

Lionel Messi kicks the soccer ball.

Goal! He is a soccer superstar.

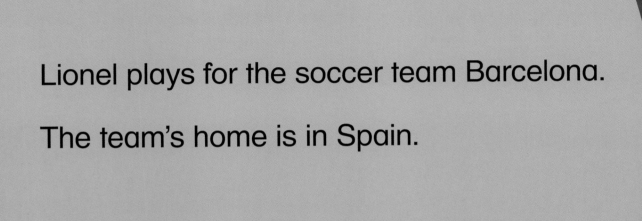

Lionel plays for the soccer team Barcelona.

The team's home is in Spain.

Lionel grew up in Argentina.

He began playing soccer as

a young boy.

He was shorter than most other players.

But he was fast and smart.

How do players help one another during games?

11

Lionel and his family moved to Spain when he was thirteen years old. He practiced soccer and grew strong.

Lionel began playing for Barcelona in 2004. He became the youngest player ever to score for the team.

Barcelona and Lionel became champions. They won Spain's top league many times.

Why do teams try to become champions?

Lionel played for Argentina in the World Cup. He tried to make them world champions.

Lionel is one of the best scorers in the world. He wants to win even more soccer games!

Soccer Gear

jersey

cleats

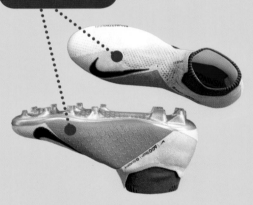

shorts

soccer ball

Picture Glossary

league

a group of teams that compete with one another

practiced

did something many times to get better at it

scorers

players who score goals

World Cup

a worldwide soccer competition

Read More

Derr, Aaron. *Soccer: An Introduction to Being a Good Sport.* Egremont, MA: Red Chair, 2017.

Flynn, Brendan. *Soccer Time!* Minneapolis: Lerner Publications, 2017.

Flynn, Brendan. *Superstars of the World Cup.* Minneapolis: Pop, 2018.

Index

Photo Credits

Image credits: Quality Sport Images/Contributor/Getty Images, pp. 5, 21, 23 (bottom left); NurPhoto/Contributor/Getty Images, p. 6; Lars Baron/Staff/Getty Images, p. 9; Luis Bagu/Stringer/Getty Images, p. 10; LLUIS GENE/Staff/Getty Images, pp. 13, 17, 23 (top left), 23 (top right); Michael Regan—EMPICS/Contributor/Getty Images, p. 14; Dokshin Vlad/Shutterstock.com, pp. 18, 23 (bottom right); eNjoy iStyle/Shutterstock.com, p. 22 (shorts); xiaorui/Shutterstock.com, p. 22 (jersey); Nattawit Khomsanit/Shutterstock.com, p. 22 (cleats); irin-k/Shutterstock.com, p. 22 (soccer ball).

Cover: Ivan Arlandis/Contributor/Getty Images.